"Quick, effective motivational & marketing messages driving you to success"

Sell Your Soul For Security

Vol. 19 In The *Sub 4 Minute Extra Mile* Series

by

Dr. Ted Ciuba

Sell Your Soul For Security

Vol. 19 In The *Sub 4 Minute Extra Mile* Series

ISBN: 978-1478115205

by **Ted Ciuba**

www.ThinkRich.com
info@holomagic.com
Parthenon Marketing Inc
2400 Crestmoor Rd #36
Nashville TN 37215   USA

Orders & Enrollments
+1-877- *4 RICHES*
***
phone +1-615-662-3169
fax: +1-615-369-9749

 Contact Ted Ciuba about speaking for or training your group or organization.

Ted Ciuba is also the author of the incredible modernization and empowerment of Napoleon Hill's success classic, *Think & Grow Rich!*

Best Books
Award
FINALIST!
USA Book News

Ted Ciuba
The New Think & Grow Rich
Author of Sub 4 Minute Extra Mile Series
Author of *The New Think And Grow Rich*

Midwest Book Review

Tamara Doris

T.J. Rohleder

"This is **more than just a revamp with modern examples** - it radically transforms the vision by adding new gender, cross-cultural and international issues to the mix, including new material to include both science and genetics, as in the Quantum reality of accelerating income and wealth.

An excellent re-do of a classic financial inspirational guide."

"The writing is so much more applicable and understandable that I am literally forcing my friends, colleagues, and mastermind members to get their copies now!

Every page fills me with passion and revs me up!"

"I picked up Ted's book -- AND I WAS SHOCKED AND AMAZED! I sat there and began going through it ... and all of a sudden looked up and over 3 hours had gone by!!! I quickly read it from cover to cover within 2 days and then turned around and did it again! Ted has done a truly amazing thing, by totally re-writing this powerful classic. Every entrepreneur and business owner simply MUST have Ted's book!"

TABLE OF CONTENTS

CONTENTS

Vol. 19 In *The Sub 4 Minute Extra Mile* Series

SELL YOUR SOUL FOR SECURITY

by

Dr. Ted Ciuba

Introduction: It Takes So Little To Excel

As an achiever, would you agree with me that you must go the extra mile? *I thought so...*

Surely you know if you do what average people do, you'll get the same kind of average results they do. And something tells me you're a cut above that!

And it's actually quite easy to stand out, because most people wouldn't dream of going the extra mile. But for you and me, while, yes, it takes something extra, yes, it takes drive and discipline.... The amazing thing is, it takes so *little* to excel!

Roger Bannister
Runs Sub 4 Minute Mile

After all, it's called the extra *mile*, not the extra *100 miles!*

Be that as it may, we're talking about the positive rewards that come to you in any economy by going the extra mile.

It was Roger Bannister who defied and redefined history by running the sub 4 minute mile.

And the amazing thing is that Bannister did NOT spend the countless hours and hours practicing that conventional training would guide him to. He gave it what he could... In his busy pre-med Oxford schedule he took a mere 30 minutes out of his daily lunch hour to train and run. And with that he set a world record that had towered 3,000 years!

He ushered in a new era of possibility. Though no one had *ever* broken it, within 2 1/2 years time of Bannister's record-breaking, seemingly unachievable sub 4 minute mile, 18 others were doing it.

And how did he do it?... It wasn't a function of *time*. Conventional sports training encompasses hours on an almost daily basis, not 30 minutes!!

It was *intention*. Roger Bannister, in the short, focused, regular, intense, intended few minutes per day he wrested from his busy Oxford pre-med studies was throwing himself into the sport. He gave it everything he could, as an additional interest and pursuit in his life...

You see, when Roger Bannister suffered the ignominious defeat of coming in 5th place in the 1952 Olympics, right then and there, he determined to be the first human to run the sub 4 minute mile!

It was just a "thought". It's just another instance and undisputable illustration, my friend, of the power of intention powered by determination.

Moments before 6 pm on 6 May 1954, he takes a breath of vision and determination. He feels it! He confides to his pacemakers "The sub 4 minute attempt is on!"

Short moments later the shot is fired... The runners are off!! Roger Bannister breaks the string at the end of the mile in 3 minutes, 59 seconds, and 4/10's, trailblazing into the sub 4 minute mile age!

Recognition Point!! - This was NOT an unintended event! Recognition point!! Little efforts, little accomplishments - short, focused, regular, intense, intended training sessions - gear into colossal events!

Also note how little it takes to stand waaay beyond the competition! Roger Bannister redefined history in one evening... And he did it only with the razor's edge of difference, 1/10 of a second over 1/2 of a second!!!

This didn't happen by circumstance... Roger Bannister didn't "drift" over the finish line into the annals of history... It was the thing he geared all his intentions to accomplish, even though he didn't spend hours and hours a day in the quest to achieve it.

Which gives rise to the name of this series, The *Sub 4 Minute Extra Mile* Series...

Now you, honoring Roger Bannister's history-setting accomplishments and methods, can make the same kind of history-breaking progress in sub 4 minutes a day! Defy the status quo in short, focused, regular, intense, intended training sessions and redefine what's possible and what you accomplish!

BULLISH NOW

You *can* compare being successful with playing a game. Let's take a football game— whether American-style or soccer-style, it doesn't really matter. That's a game in which you have to be good to compete at the higher levels, and where you take it *seriously*.

And the interesting thing about it is the rewards we talk about for the winners – in music, in sports, in politics, and in business - are *huge*. The paybacks to the participants who don't win are paltry.

It's a decision that makes itself, things being what they are, you go for the winner's side. The same thing is true when you play Monopoly. It seems like certain people usually get the hotels. You want to be on the winner's side.

Another interesting thing is, you cannot play any game without the risk of loss. It's inherent, so you must risk loss. Interestingly though, *usually,* as you've heard the saying, a battle does not the war make.

In other words, not every single promotion you do is going to work like *gangbusters*. Sales at the front line is the ultimate proving ground. You're usually making it profitable off a very small group of potential prospects converted into buyers.

But if you stay after it, if you stay focused, if you know exactly what you're going for and why, if you're determined to get it, knowing you *will* because of what you *do...* Almost unerringly, eventually, you will.

Well, weather a few upsets - Call them the "gusts of the single day". Hey, look at any stock chart or any options, commodities, or currency charts. It's full of lines going up and down all the time. Sometimes it gets congested, sometimes it makes a breakaway on news events.

Your human experience will not be different, but you can be bullish if you direct it that way, and that's what I wish for you. Be bullish on your career; be bullish on your success. As you are, you're doing the right things the right way the right day—*now*! It always comes down to *action!*

Not every "day" or every event or promotion will be a winner, but you are the one who can make sure the trend is moving upward.

NOTES

Item / passage / page	Insight	Action

FINANCIAL LITERACY EQUALS FINANCIAL LEVERAGE

You really can't blame people for getting it all *screwed up*. They have been taught that way, and we are *social animals* and we learn from our environment—I mean, this is nature. However, it's just numerically the case that they were born in that relationship, in that family, in that city, in that society. The truth is absolutely different.

What am I referring to? I am referring to how you're taught and trained to get a job; taught, trained and educated to get a job.

And you're taught, trained and educated that you can get a *better* job if you want to make more money and have more of the comforts of life, when in fact there isn't a job that will ever do it for you. A job, which some people say is an acronym for "just over broke," is, as a matter of fact, what most people are.

What are we talking about? This: it means being in business for yourself. But not just any business. Many business "owners" simply traded their job for a "pay yourself last" chain around their neck.. That could be worse than a job. You've got to get away from trading hours for dollars.

"Oh, this is a good job. It pays $20 an hour." (Adjust this figure for your own location and time.)

You think so? Hey, on an eight-hour day that's $160. Now, you can convert that to your own currency, but then by the time you pay 40-50% to the tax person, that ain't a good job!

And what are you going to do? Are you going to put in a little bit of overtime? How much can you do, and how much do you want to do? You've got to think *leverage*. You've got to think multiplication.

What can you do, for instance, like a rock star or an information marketer, just once and have it sell over and over again? What can you create, in the Internet Age of course, that's digital and when you sell it anywhere in the world, you've still got it and you can sell it again?

Think multiplication, think leverage, think like a business owner. Think, what can you leverage?

You can be sure that Henry Ford, had he stayed an *employee* instead of *employing* thousands and thousands... You can be sure that Andrew Carnegie, had he stayed an employee instead of employing thousands and thousands... Neither would never have found the leverage and gone on to the great wealth and benefit they brought to the world.

It is no discredit to be an employee if you're getting educated, getting motivated, determining the insight, creating a strategy to get out of it. Think leverage. Think multiplication. Think, what can you do once—design a system, patent something, copyright something—then have it sell forever or a long time? What can you get other people's money to do for you?

Think, think, think like a businessperson. Financial literacy comes into the life of every person who achieves success. No, you don't have to keep the books. No, you don't have to do all the micro-managing... But you've got to be involved. The business depends on the direction and the energy you give it. That being the case, *jump in!*

SELL YOUR SOUL FOR SECURITY

Well, it happened again this morning.

At a certain enterprise in Nashville, which will remain unnamed, the management showed up early and told 200 employees—now, I know we're not talking giant numbers here, we're talking principles—that their services were no longer needed.

"Oh, sorry that your retirement plan will be screwed up. Oh, you didn't get vested, and I'm sorry about a few other things. And, you know, your pay stops immediately. Sorry I didn't get to notify you in advance and give you six months to plan it out." Not that most people would have prepared, because historically even in situations where people have been notified, they didn't.

That's just one example; you can provide hundreds of them yourself, and if you want to get big numbers, then you've got the auto manufacturers, financial institutions, great appliance companies, computer firms, airlines and oil industries that lay off 10,000 or 20,000 at a time.

The irony of this, always, in my industry—helping to make people independent, helping turn people into entrepreneurs and business people, where they can leverage and multiply their wealth and actually *get ahead* instead of just running a little bit further and at *a little bit* higher level in the rat race—is that they're still bound in the rat race.

The biggest thing I run against is the need for security; the need for *benefits*.

Now, granted, if you're like one particular friend I have who is 48, he and his wife are both in massively bad health—I'm not even going to mention what part lifestyle might have played in that—but he's not going to be productive in a business.

He just doesn't have the energy, the stamina, the drive, the get up and go; it's already got up and gone. In that one case, it might be acceptable to get a job.

Everything else—the security is an *illusion*. It's something they *sold* you on, and something you have bought into! You *can* undo it! You know, insurance doesn't cost very much. Getting ahead doesn't cost that much. But you know what? Selling your soul for security doesn't offer any security, either. Sure, there is risk in everything.

The trick is in choosing the right set of risks —

Therefore, why don't you choose the rewards you would like to have and go after them? Let the whiners and the wannabes take the risks of the company they work for not needing them any longer, maybe at a crucial time when they don't really feel like going out in the work force again and they're not prepared for retirement.

You, great soul, aware you can't risk *not* moving on the deepest dreams of your heart, not knowing to what glorious vision fulfilled they might lead you to, jump into conscious, dedicated action.

It's not about work, because you'll work either way. It might include fulfillment and actualization. Don't sell your soul for security. *Choose* the rewards you would like to have, and go after them!

THE DIFFERENCE BETWEEN ACHIEVERS AND NORMAL PEOPLE: FOCUS

What is the difference between achievers and normal people? Well, it's not brainpower. It's not time. It's not race, sex, religion. There is something, though. There's a razor's edge of difference.

Let me give you an example. Right now one of my primary home towns is Nashville, Tennessee, otherwise known as Music City USA, a town of musicians. It's in our culture, it's in our blood. It's our stew. We know the business.

Interestingly enough, in that business there are multimillionaires whom you surely know about. Garth Brooks might come to mind. Alan Jackson and Dolly Parton are media darlings. Then there are seemingly hundreds of thousands of songwriters and musicians, enough to comprise a whole city, who are barely skating by, barely making it. We call them "driving on maypops"—those bald tires they're driving may pop any minute.

What is the difference? Look, time isn't it! A lot of times talent isn't it, either. It's focus! It's intention. It's determination. It's daring! The successful ones know what they're doing, design the path, and they go after it. They take that extra mile—they take what they're doing seriously. They take action relentlessly. They don't just talk about it.

It's situational acuity—they always know if what they're doing is improving them or is not. Then they have the discipline and courage, the decision, to do what they need to do. They "look" like they are doing the same things, but they're going for more and they're responsible to it.

That's the difference I wish for you.

NOTES

Item / passage / page	Insight	Action

CONSIDER THE CONSEQUENCES OF NOT FOLLOWING THROUGH ON YOUR DREAMS

One of the things you want to do is motivate yourself to do what you need to do. Will you have to take some risks in doing what you're doing? Yeah, you always will. You *always* will. For instance, I quit my job before I had replaced my income. I felt like I needed that extra time to make it happen; I felt like it *would* happen.

Am I recommending that to you? Don't be insane. Am I saying *don't* do such a thing? No, I'm not. I'm saying have confidence. I'm saying you can do what you want to do. But here's what I use to motivate me.

I say, "Wow! I can *stay* in this boredom, I can *stay* in this situation that's really not productive, that's really not me, where I'm really not helping other people, or I can get active, take a few risks, and make happen what I want to have happen."

You see that confidence?: *"I can make happen what I want to have happen"*. You can.

One of the things I use to motivate me is the consequences I'll be living with if I *don't* act on my dreams. These are so horrible, so totally unacceptable, that I *can not dream* of not rising to the occasion. That's what I wish for you.

You know, any warrior takes risks. I often mention how I love the stories of King Arthur and the Knights of the Round Table. One of those knights, Sir Lancelot, a consummate warrior, took a lot of risks. And one time when Queen Guinevere was in danger—she'd been kidnapped by a brutish *miscreant*—Sir Lancelot chased after him without a thought for his own safety.

The miscreant had armor; Sir Lancelot had none. But the value of the prize was worth everything, and the consequences of *not* following through were horrific.

You know this miscreant had *unhealthy desires* for the *queenly fine* young Guinevere. He had every intention of ravishing her. And time, *time*, was the only thing that stood between that ugly event happening and Sir Lancelot wasted no time and took every risk to make a rescue happen instead.

So consider the consequences of not following through on your goals, dreams, and ambitions, and you'll get a bit more motivation.

NOTES

Item / passage / page	Insight	Action

NOTHING'S WRONG—THOSE ARE GROWING PAINS

Do you remember growing up? I know my mother taught me, and I assume it's a universal phenomenon, those pains I was feeling were "growing pains". "Nothing's wrong, honey, those are growing pains."

And you know, I think about that from time to time—and about how, as humans, we're pretty much afraid of change, afraid of growth, afraid of doing something that doesn't feel natural. The problem with that is that a lot of times, what seems natural only seem natural because it's so common it's turned stale. We're not growing.

Give me the growing pains any day. *Embrace* the growing pains.

You see, change happens on the edge—that's where the growth is. It is new territory... We *are* stretching and becoming more. And it takes a little bit of uncertainty, a little bit of balance, a little bit of exploration, a little bit of being an explorer and a leader. I suggest you figure out at the edge is where the growth is.

Once you do that, you're committed, because you yearn for that new level. You're willing to follow your instincts no matter how much noise may enter with the Cosmic intuitions that are guiding you...

You've heard of the chrysalis that grows into the butterfly. Of course I can't get in his head, but I can bet you the ugly pupa doesn't know that this uncertainty and metamorphosis it's in, this period of darkness, is going to end with it becoming one of most beautiful creatures in Nature.

That's what growth can be for you. It takes you to new places, makes you a newer, higher, better, further contributing person.

I wish it for you.

NOTES

Item / passage / page	Insight	Action

PHOTOS ALLOW US TO RE-LIVE THE RICHNESS

I'm coming to you as a friend and confidante today. I've just experienced a little session where I had some emotional engagement with some photos and video footage. I compared a golden lab I had, Helen, with Henry Ford, saying she wasn't afraid to jump on something and get it done. There's video footage of her running along side a Ford pickup at 30 mph…

But be that as it may, and this is the important point, it has brought up a vital demonstration of the power and value of photos, videos, articles, and everything else we do to commemorate and make a permanent record of ourselves… The value that they do have.

It goes beyond that. Of course I don't remember the photo of Henry Ford when it was taken, and of course I don't remember one of my favorite photos, of Roger Bannister crossing the line in 3:59:04, when it was taken. Yet those things have an internal memory, a groove in my psychic consciousness – programmed there by photos another person took.

It's like Carl Jung talks about: the collective unconscious. Those things have a tremendous impact on me. We are all the same at deeper, profound, Quantum field reality. And I'm suspecting they have an impact on you, also.

And the video footage of my dog, the photo of my two Panamanian loves – wife and daughter published on the cover of the book, *Celebrate Today!*, the Christmas photos of my two daughters together - from two different families in 12 different poses. Wow!

Photos allow us to re-live the richness again and again! I even get sad talking about this joy we get to re-live the richness again.

NOTES

Item / passage / page	Insight	Action

ONCE DEPARTED, THERE IS NO COMING BACK

Featuring Edward Fitzgerald

Edward Fitzgerald translated about 1,000 poems from Ancient Persia written in the 11th and 12th centuries. He called it *The Rubaiyat of Omar Khayyam,* and one of the main themes in it is that you have to live *now.*

Now, because life passes so fast, and once departed, there is no coming back.

So let me read a few verses to you to illustrate the meaning they have for us as marketers, as people who are making a positive contribution—although that wasn't necessarily the original theme.When it was originally written, it was, "live fast, love hard because you're going to die. Enjoy! Enjoy!"

We talk about *produce, produce.*

> *Here with a loaf of bread beneath the bough,*
> *A flask of wine, a book of verse and thou*
> *Beside me singing in the wilderness—*
> *And wilderness is paradise enow.*

In other words, here we are—you, me, a book of verse, a loaf of bread, wine, you're singing, playing, and this *is* paradise.

We translate everything we see, find, encounter into our language, into our ethics, our forces.

> *"How sweet is mortal sovranty!"-- think some;*
> *Others -- "How blest the Paradise to come!"*
> *Ah, take the cash in hand and waive the rest;*
> *Oh, the brave music of a distant drum!*

Don't be the fool listening to the promises of distant drums… How easy it is to be brave and to make posturing proclamations so many legions from the battle. Don't be a fool, it is what it is.

> *Dreaming when dawn's left hand was in the sky*
> *I heard a voice within the tavern cry,*
> *"Awake, my little ones, and fill the cup*
> *Before life's liquor in its cup be dry."*

Drink the cup now, fill the cup now, it's going to be dry.

> *And, as the cock crew, those who stood before*
> *The tavern shouted -- "Open then the door!*
> *You know how little while we have to stay,*
> *And, once departed, may return no more."*

Advice from ancient Persia to you. Live life to the max today, produce, create, love, and let those you love know that you love them today. It is urgent. Once departed, you may return no more.

PEOPLE WHO ARE WINNERS MADE THEMSELVES WINNERS

Let's call a spade a spade. In an entrepreneurial environment, a lot of times the question is, "Well, can we do this?" I'm here to tell you there's an attitude that you can adopt and winners have adopted. Because, in this cause and effect reality we live in, the people who are winners *made themselves winners*.

It's a paradigm something like this... They don't ask *if* something can be done, they ask *how* it can be done. Once they figure out they want something, they just figure out how to get it. "I'd like this new project. I'd like this new boat. I'd like this new house. I'd like to vacation. I'd like to put a new section on the house."

They don't get stuck in *I don't have that kind of money and the bank won't loan me any*. They ask, "How do I get that?" And then they go to work producing it.

That's what I wish for you.

NOTES

Item / passage / page	Insight	Action

PANAMA JOHN HAD IT COMING

Panama John had it coming. Hey friends, this is Panama Ted (http://PanamaTed.com), your friend Ted Ciuba. And even though I'm coming to you now, I'm in Nashville, you do know that I have a place and I have a wife, and I have a child, in Panamá. I actually live between the two countries Nashville and La Ciudad de Panamá.

Who's Panama John? Well, if you were a UK citizen you would know, and if you were a Panama ex-pat like I am you would know, the rest of the people don't really know. Wasn't generally newsworthy elsewhere.

But what it was, was an insurance fraud. He faked his death - got on a boat, paddled out to the North Sea and actually lived hidden in his house, in another room, with a fake entrance and a wall, for a long time. And the wreckage of his small boat washed up to shore at the appropriate time and place some weeks later to corroborate the story...

And somehow or another he got a fake/false identity. Got a passport, got to Panamá, got fascinated with it and got his wife to collect the insurance proceeds - this was some years down the road. They kept the charade up pretty good, and they bought a place in Panamá.

Everything Panama John was doing was fraudulent!

I don't know how isolated and how segmented some peoples' minds think the world is, so let a man who's crisscrossed the world a dozen times give you some perspective. Getting around the world – while it may require airplanes, hotels, and rental cars or jeeps instead of just a monitor and a mouse – is no more difficult than getting around the World Wide Web. I mean get hold of it, there is no place to hide. Everywhere is as convenient as anywhere.

Honesty is the best policy.

And as my friend and buddy, an ex P. I. (private investigator) likes to say, "Everybody always makes a mistake."

So what did this idiot do?

First of all let's forget about all the crime, the fraudulent activity, and the way that forced him to live and the way it was bound to come - again, telling you, you can't live that way. And then they buy a place with the insurance proceeds. They're a happy couple. They pose together as purchasers. The real estate agent puts them on his website as a testimonial. And life still seems to happily go on.

Overly sensitive to the criminal insurance scam, Panama John, plugged in from his cozy air-conditioned apartment on the south coast of Panamá, couldn't live with it anymore. He shivers in fear are about to find him... This is a common characteristic that gets amateur criminals... They say a lot of them - fraudsters, child molesters, to tax evaders - when they get to a point where they're absolutely afraid they're about to be discovered, jailed and everything, they actually turn themselves in.

Paranoia runs deep.

They come forward themselves. And that's what he did. But it was with a story of amnesia. "Where have I been these last eight years? Last thing I remember, I was paddling out to the North Sea." Of course that story didn't hold up too well. Not too long.

Some citizen in the UK went to the web, went to Google probably, although I don't know that fact, typed in his name, "John Darwin" and typed in the word "Panama" and surfed straight to the photo of the smiling fugitive couple thinking they were far enough away in Panamá to be isolated from events back home.

Panama John had it coming, another reason why I say about success and thriving, it's not really about morality and ethics... While, it definitely is in my life, I'm telling you, more than that, it's about honesty is the best *policy*. If you want to get along in this world you *will* be moral, and ethical, and treat everybody with respect. And you'll never try and commit, knowingly, a fraudulent act like Panama John.

TRADING AWAY EVERYTHING FOR INSTANT GRATIFICATION

Those of you who know me know I've admitted I'm not Christian. However, by the way, I *have* read the entire Christian Bible cover-to-cover numerous times. I *majored* in romantic and epic literature, and it's got a lot of good stories.

So I'm not proselytizing here when I feature a story from that amazing book. I'm telling you wisdom; I'm sharing something with you to give you insight, which is what that whole book's about, by the way.

There's a story in there about Jacob and Esau, two brothers. Esau is much more active, much more warrior-like, much more of the world. He's been out hunting. Isaac, their father, the patriarch, is about to pass on. He knows his days are numbered.

And back in those days, estates and power were passed on with the paternal blessing to the eldest son, being Esau. Jacob was more of a book-learner, more of a *romantic* man, more of the *poet*. Hey, too bad, Jacob—you're son number 2.

So Esau comes in from the fields, and Jacob had been in his study, writing poetry.

Esau roars, "G*ive me something to* eat! I am famished! I am *famished!"*

Jacob says, "Well, I have a mess of porridge here" (which is kind of like a stew).

"Give it to me! Give it to me now! I'm about to die," thunders Esau.

Jacob says, "Well, I will if you will trade me your patrimony."

Esau replies, "*I will do it! I must eat now or I will die! My patrimony is now yours!"*

He eats like crazy. He scarfs it up, belches, and is satisfied.

Jacob enters the candlelit room with the blind, dying Isaac, and receives the blessing and the wealth. From that single slop of porridge, it came to Jacob to be father of the tribe from which descends the modern Jewish race.

What's the message here? The message here is that Jacob had a long-term view. Jacob was crafty… Jacob used his head. Esau was living like an animal, lacking the wisdom to use the human animal's higher abilities. He was of the *moment*. Esau wanted *instant gratification*! Isn't that exactly what it was?

And he traded away every single thing he had in his life for it. And he had the sooo much. He had, after all, the massive patrimony of his father.

Which one do you want to be—Jacob or Esau?

I suggest a lot of people die from cancer because they opted continuously for instant gratification. Every puff they took, they knew they were killing themselves, but it felt good in the moment. Choosing the short term good – even if it's really bad – over the long-term right choice. That's the definition of instant gratification.

Same thing with obese people, diabetes sufferers, and high blood pressure cases – in most instances healthier, alternative lifestyles exist over the ones which got them to where they are... And they brought it all on themselves, trading away everything for instant gratification.

I suggest a lot of people who die broke were going for instant gratification. You know, *"How can I save and invest if I can't even pay my bills now?"*

Much less learn how to invest... Much less get a little grubstake and let it grow with compounding interest. Much less create a product, a niche, a business that might have a life of its own, that could provide necessary residual income...

There's a big difference in the results you get between instant gratification and long-term commitment.

I know you'll make the right choice.

TRAVEL BROADENS THE INDIVIDUAL

They say travel broadens an individual. Indeed it does. You see customs are different, and you just see different preferences. Laws are always different in different places. Traffic is different, as are the values that people have, the way they relate to one another. You see things.

It's true. Travel broadens one. Travel makes a person complete. That's why, for a lot of people, it's considered part of the educational process. When they're getting their education, they're sent off to a foreign country for a while to get some education there.

We just recently had six of us sitting around the table. We were in Panamá, and Panamá is the crossroads of the world. Obviously there's the Panamá Canal—everybody knows about that.

But also it's the gateway between North and South America. It has been *for thousands and thousands of years*. It's a little isthmus, 50 miles wide at its narrowest point.

We're at Royal Decameron Resort on the Pacific coast, approximately 100 miles west of Panama City. I look up and there are six of us representing five sovereign nations at a single table. I think *"Wow!"* We're all having a conversation, having a great time. The only language we could speak in common was Spanish, so we were speaking in Spanish.

One person was from Canada—Montreal, Quebec. Normally his life is in French. Another person was from the UK. His life is in English—English with an accent, I say tongue-in-cheek, because England is where English originated, even though Americans think they have an accent, and it kind of offends them.

How do we know that? Well, travel broadens one, right?

One lady was from the Nöbe Buglé Indian tribe. When she visits her mother—her father passed away recently... When she drives away, there is no contact. In the Indian village where she lives, there is no phone service. Cell service doesn't reach there. No electricity. No indoor plumbing. No automobile roads. She, of course, has her language, too.

At the resort, the only language we all have in common is Spanish.

Then there's me, representing the US, speaking English, of course; and my wife, who's from Panamá, and she, of course, speaks English, too—she's connected with an American. And then my mother-in-law, who is the only one who hasn't been moving and traveling outside of Panamá, the only one who is not actively bi-lingual.

It's just real interesting how you can get six people together from five different nations, with six different points of view—and do you think you *might* get a little insight, a little education, a little delight? A little information that might really help you as you take your next step? Some exchanges that can't help but make you a more knowledgeable, interesting, capable person?...

It's a no-brainer. We say the same thing about reading, or the Discovery Channel. The more we know, the better off we are. We're not talking about wasting time, we're talking about *using* time to make ourselves a better person.

Travel definitely broadens your outlook, and therefore it gives more power to everything you do.

IT'S ALL ABOUT GETTING THE EDGE

Featuring Tom Justin

When I was speaking with my colleague Tom Justin about HoloMagic recently, he told me,

> "It's like magic. I love your concept and the *HoloMagic* and what you put together. And you literally have this holographic universe of opportunity, possibilities, education, life experience, business experience.
>
> "When people put themselves in that receptive state and they want to start magnetizing, for instance, they'll go to your website, they'll look at something and they'll think, 'Well, that has no relevance to me,' and they'll click on it, a drop-down menu comes down, and they go, 'Oh, what is that?'
>
> "And they find a piece of information that they either didn't know would be important, or that they'd been looking for.
>
> "That happens in our lives all the time. Activate awareness, and then activation starts to bring this edge—this bigger edge or, as I call it, the wizard's edge, closer to us in our daily lives."

Indeed. One of the stories I often share is one I wrote in an article called "That's How HoloMagic Works." It was a story of a lady, a good friend, who solicited me about using her new startup fulfillment center.

For those who aren't educated, that means to send out books, tapes, audios, DVDs, CDs, that we all do. And so I told her, "Well, yeah. I will. But I'm not going to take anything away from anybody else. Everything is running smoothly. Next time I need you, *I will*."

Lo and behold, I developed a product which happened to be *The NEW Think and Grow Rich* Audio Version.

But you know, I like the Internet very much because I don't have to use fulfillment.

So here I put this product up, digital only. You download it, and I put up a sales letter and rocket- launched it. The very first order that came in, however, the person wrote me an email back after they received their receipt, and said, "Don't you have this in physical form?" That helped that lady who had the fulfillment center, because I gave her my business.

But what we didn't see happening behind the scenes was that the night before, she was praying. She was meditating, she was tuned into the Cosmic, the HoloCosm, and she basically put a challenge up and said, "I need to know if this is right, and the only way I'll know if this is right is if tomorrow Ted gives me an order for fulfillment."

To that, Tom said:

> "Wow, it seems so strange to people who haven't had the experience or, at least, aren't consciously aware they've had the experience. Everybody has them, but many are not consciously aware that they've had the experiences which they've had.
>
> That works. That really works. Does it work all the time? Does it work every time? Is it perfect?
>
> *"Absolutely not*! But again*, it's all about having the edge,* and when we use these techniques in our daily lives, and with greater and greater frequency, our edge increases.
>
> "I'm not much of a gambler. I live in Las Vegas, and they didn't build all these high rises with winners. But the edge that gamblers take, they get just one little piece of a point, a percentage point, and they can increase their winnings tremendously when they know how to do certain things.
>
> "I can't give you even a quotient example in gambling, but I remember reading about this guy who gambled millions of dollars a year, and was quite successful at his gambling. He knew all the edge that he could take. He knew he could get increased odds if he bet a certain way.
>
> The average gambler doesn't use any of this stuff, and that's who builds the high rises for these people. But the few people who have the edge and study it and know it, use it to become winners. And it's the same in business; it's the same in personal lives. We find our edge. Where can we find our edge?"

It's *all* about getting the edge, Tom Justin. I like that.

THE FIVE BIGGEST MISTAKES YELLOW PAGES ADVERTISERS MAKE

Featuring Larry Cohn

Hi! My name is Larry Cohn with Instant Yellow Page Profits, and Ted has asked me to give you some information about marketing and about Yellow Pages and print advertising. That's my area of expertise, and what I specialize in. So here's the five biggest mistakes yellow pages advertisers make.

The first big mistake people make with Yellow Page and print advertising is using their business name as a headline. You should never use your business name as a headline. It's a terrible mistake. It contains no *benefits*, and that's what people are looking for when they're scanning headlines to see if they're going to read what's below it.

So what you want to do is have two or three of the strongest benefits that your ideal target prospect is looking for in your headline.

Then it's a really good idea to have some sort of risk reversal or guarantees, so you can have a personal promise or a guarantee in the ad that tells what level of service they can expect, how you're going to assure their satisfaction, and those sorts of things. Not having one is the second biggest mistake.

The third biggest mistake is a lot of people make mistakes in bullet points in their print and Yellow Page advertising. They list, maybe, the fancy new machine, the XYZ 90 that they just bought and they spent a lot of money on and they're very proud to own—but that means nothing, because that's a feature, not a benefit.

What you want to do is convert your bullet points from features to benefits. So if the XYZ 90 machine stretches your back and you are a chiropractor and it gets people to avoid doing surgery, then that's the benefit. So those are the things you want to be highlighting in your bullet points.

The fourth biggest mistake is a lot of people do image advertising. But you need to have a good *Direct Response* ad, which is the type of advertising you should be doing— not image or branding if you're a very small company. It takes far too much money to build an image or brand. It's going to take hundreds of millions of dollars, so you want to be using *Direct Response* advertising.

An ad is not a *Direct Response* ad unless it has an offer. So you want to have a really great offer—this is what causes the prospect to get knocked off the fence. They may be evaluating a couple of different situations, and deciding who they're going to call or who they want to hire.

If you have a great new client welcome offer, then that's going to exceed the offer that everybody else has in their ads. The odds are they have no offer. That welcomes the person in, knocks them off the fence of indecision, gets them to call you. And then once that phone rings, as a small businessman it's your job to convert them to a sale.

And finally, the fifth biggest mistake yellow page advertisers make relates to color in the ad. A lot of the Yellow Pages sales reps really talk about color. Typically they'll double the cost of the ad for color. They'll tell you you have to have color or people won't respond—and the studies I've seen conducted outside their industry dispute that.

Really what you want is contrast, so a lot of times you can just go with a bigger ad in black-and-white, and avoid having all the color charges and a smaller ad. So that would be my advice—to go ahead with the black that has good contrast with the background, and is easily read and legible.

Those are my tips for today, the five biggest mistakes yellow page advertisers make.

THE LITMUS TEST

People sometimes ask, "How do I know if I'm in a good partnership?" or "How do I know if I'm in a true MasterMind?"

There are a lot of different things to this, and this is just a short article. I don't have time to go into everything; we're not teaching a course. And it really *does* merit a course. In fact, I've taken some of those in Communications, at the doctorate level.

But one of the really relevant characteristics I just call the litmus test. It's simple, but it's accurate. It's just this: If something bad happens to you, something bad happens to me. If something bad happens to me, something bad happens to you. If something good happens to me, something good happens to you. If something good happens to you, something good happens to me.

That's how you know if you're connected at that level we call the MasterMind, because you rely so much on that other person—again, whether it's a stereotypical marital relationship, which applies, or whether it's a business relationship at the level we're talking about. This is where if something bad happens to either person it *is* bad for the team, it *is* bad for the effort.

Now, does it mean that we won't survive and carry on, and even thrive? No, of course you know it doesn't mean that, because that would be contrary to the philosophy we teach.

But it does definitely mean that you have a care, and a concern. Sometimes you recognize that you have a care and concern about the other party or parties, and you need to realize the other party or parties have that same concern about you. You need to, and you want to, give them as much consideration as you can.

Why? Because you want to receive as much consideration as you can. Now, in a MasterMind that's fully functioning and healthy, that's probably working fine. On the other hand, many of us looking to develop that are looking for a litmus test. One of the ways you know you're connected is if when something either good or bad happens to the other any party, it translates into good or bad for all other parties.

Now, it doesn't happen if you're working for the state, and the person at the desk next to you gets in a horrible auto accident, dies, or is permanently disfigured. That's a tragedy. Wish to God it didn't happen. But, other than feelings of sentiment and knowing the person, it doesn't affect you. They're going to replace that person; they've probably already got a ton of applicants, right?

Now, on the other hand, if your marriage partner or your business partner, someone who's in a complementary relationship in which you're depending on each other, where the two of you are working together as a team—if one of you disappears, then it *is* a stress on you. Emotionally, it's much deeper than with all the other affairs of life; much deeper.

So, try that litmus test. It's a very powerful indicator. If something bad happens to a person I'm connected with, that's a measure—because if it's bad to me if something bad happens to them, I know we're connected at that level. Or if something bad happens to me and it's bad for them, the same. If something good happens to me, something good happens to them. If something good happens to them, something good happens to me.

Just another piece of the litmus test.

THE INTERNET MAKES IT AFFORDABLE TO BUILD A RELATIONSHIP

Featuring Jeff Gardner

Recently I spoke with a man who has been a mail order maven. His name is Jeff Gardner—you may have heard of him through *Wealth World*. Recently, he's been moving more and more towards the Internet. Here's why, in his own words:

> **Jeff Gardner:** I'm working more on the Internet for a lot of different reasons. I think marketing should be all about marketing, so I'm still always going to keep direct mail in the mix. But I really like the Internet, because you get to touch people a lot more, many more times, for a lot less money.
>
> I like the ability to go back to people over and over again. Because in direct mail, you can touch people, but you're not able to build up that relationship. Everything really has to be kind of a selling proposition, if you're going to be able to continue to afford to mail to people.
>
> This is versus online marketing, where you have the ability to e-mail people on a regular basis, show them free videos and then free reports, and do that without any real cost to you, building up that relationship and that bond to see your conversion rate go up.

So yeah, we've been in the mail order business for a long time, and I think its strong and always going to be a major part of our business. But the Internet is just key. It's essential to building up relationships with your customers and increasing the overall value of your entire business.

NOTES

Item / passage / page	Insight	Action

THE QUALITY OF THE DIAGNOSIS WILL DETERMINE THE QUALITY OF YOUR EVENTUAL BENEFIT

People who have never worked with a marketing consultant, or people who haven't done it in quite some time, sometimes forget. In a way, I'm a healer, you know. When things are going good, riding at the top of the world, is not usually when people come to me—but hey, if I wasn't here solving problems, what benefit would I be?

Every person who contributes any value is solving a problem, whether it's the waitress in the restaurant or whether it's the executive in the tower with a certain company. It's the same way here, too.

As a healer, a lot of times I get the impression—and I know it to be true—that people think, "Okay, I'll contact you, and I'll pay you your hourly fee, and you'll do some wizard wave and *boom*! I'll suddenly be making millions of dollars." Business and personal people think that.

Well, I wish it was that way. But think of this—think of something that you *do know,* because everybody is human. Let's say a person goes to the doctor. Let's say they're hurting in their back and are in excruciating pain. Does the doctor jump right in? Does the doctor pull out the scalpel and start cutting? *No!*

The doctor will send the person for X-rays. The doctor may do an MRI. The doctor may get some outside opinions. The doctor is going to study and evaluate things and *only* after that's happened, which they call diagnosis, will the doctor begin to prescribe a treatment program or begin to take whatever action is necessary.

Listen, as a marketing consultant, as a person who coaches personal development, it's really the same way. I need to know what you want and where you are. And you do, too. Think about this for *you*. I need to know *where* you are, what issues you have that need to be cleaned up on the way to where you want to go. And then we can easily, quickly develop plans to accomplish that.

And there's another thing few people know. Again, let's compare it with the medical profession. I know you've heard this: "Well, let's try this pill, and you take it for six days, then come back and you tell me how you feel, and how you've responded to the medication. If this doesn't do it, then we'll prescribe something else that I believe will, but I'd rather you be on this to start with."

As marketing consultant, we do the same thing. We say test, test small.

Can I guarantee direct mail will work for you? Well, almost; almost, *definitely*! Can I guarantee the very first mailing, the very first package, the very first offer we put together, the very first approach we make to your customers about what we *think* is bothering them will work?

Can't guarantee that. That's why we say test, and test small. The results *will* tell you.

See, whenever you get a good idea, *don't bet the farm*. Test and see what kind of results you get, and then you know, like the doctor, whether you should prescribe something else or stay on the path you're on.

There *is* a diagnosis period any time you want change, personal or business. Embrace it, because the quality of the diagnosis will determine the quality of your eventual benefit.

GIVE THAT NEW PROJECT THE BOOT

I often thank God I'm an optimist—thank God I over-exaggerate on the positive side. Because it's led me to do a lot of things reap a lot of rewards I might not otherwise have done.

On the other hand, we're in business; we all need to be realistic about this. We need tools and technologies, a checklist—just like a seasoned pilot, who knows how to fly, uses a checklist. We have these same things in business that help us stay on track more than we might otherwise, given our own human emotions

One of them I always call *"Let's give it the BOOT!"* Whenever, for instance, we're launching a new product, or we're launching a new sales letter, we've got goals and objectives just like anybody would. *But* we don't have just *one* set of goals and objectives, and I recommend you don't either.

We have the BOOT. We've got three goals here. The first is the *Basic*—what is it that we feel just absolute certain is a no-down knockout for us, as seasoned marketers? For us, as people who know the product we're dealing with in this market?

We'll make that the Basic, which boils down to *"We can live with this if we do this well."* This is how we expect to do if we don't hit it out of the park.

And then we have our *Objective*—what is it we *really* do want to accomplish? What numbers do we really want to get? What sales? What conversion rates are we looking for? What do we want these tests to tell us?

That's the Objective. We know, usually in dollars and cents, number of units, or key percentages exactly what we *really* want. See, the Basic is that we make money; then the Objective is what we really want.

And then, remember, we're going to give it the BOOT, we go for the *Over the Top* spot, which is what we'd love to see. What is it if we hit it over the top of the fence at the ballpark? What would make us dance, what would make us embrace in ecstasy, what would make us a lot more money? What would take us *over the top?*

And there's your BOOT: Basic, Objective, Over the Top goals.

And you know, the funny thing is I've seen many over-the-top targets get hit.

As a sound business person you strive to make sound and definite plans. Now that you know about BOOT Thinking, when setting goals and objectives, give that new project the BOOT.

THE MOST AMAZING PIECE OF PAPER

What if I was to offer to sell you a piece of paper I've carried around in my pocket that had motivated me? Would you give me a million dollars for that piece of paper? Well, could you find a million dollars, assuming you didn't have it yourself? I bet you could. I'm willing to bet you could.

The piece of paper me is torn, and I put scotch tape on it. It's tattered, and the edges are frayed. It's kind of like an old crusty dollar bill—or whatever you have in whatever nation you're in. Kind of like that.

Seem like a million dollars is too high?

And I've had it at various times in my pants pocket, in my shirt pocket. I've even had it in my wallet. And I've even left it at home when I was going into risky terrain where I didn't want to chance losing it.

And can I tell you it's actually made me a million dollars? The answer is *mas o menos*—more or less. Here's what I can tell you.

Could you find a million dollars for this old, beat-up piece of paper? I bet you could. See, it's not just a piece of paper—that's not where the value is. The condition of the paper, if the message is still readable, is of no relevance.

If you knew that ragged piece of paper was the map to a treasure of incalculable riches exceeding $10 million in value, now could you find a million dollars? Now it's an easy task, isn't it?

You could even find others who'd invest with you for a share of the profits, or interest on the money while it was lent. True? True. Case closed.

Well, I do have a piece of paper like that. You, consuming these articles is reading that piece of paper. It can be and *is* worth $10 million or more. A most amazing piece of paper. And for those reading online, it's not even physical realm paper, it's virtual paper.

But the message is timeless—the inspiration, the guidance, the education, the training, the getting your head straight, the keeping you on track, the checking up on you...all these things are worth millions for a person like you.

Yes, it's the most amazing piece of paper. Thank God you've got it, too.

NOTES

Item / passage / page	Insight	Action

Index

"You Are Closer To A Million Dollar$ Than You Now Dream!"

This is the modernized, quantum empowered version of Napoleon Hill's success classic , *Think And Grow Rich!*

#1 Best-Seller

An instruction manual to *consciously* direct the Quantum universe to manifest your positive desires."

Napoleon Hill Overlooks Ted Ciuba
Physical, Kindle. iStore

Are you ready for breakthrough progress overnight?!

Engage with *The New Think And Grow Rich* - empower yourself! Start exactly where you are - no experience, no education, no cash required! Discover how to…

- Trigger the *self-fulfilling prophecy* and the *law of attraction*!
- Apply the insights of the secret "combination" to work for your immediate, easy success
- Direct the Quantum universe to deliver success
- Unleash that powerful "HoloMagic c2 factor" to accomplish your pursuits in a fraction of the time, with only a quanta of the effort to reap HUGE, AMAZING, WINDFALL results!

Mark Whyborn, UK

*"I have read **The New Think And Grow Rich** and there is a **HUGE** improvement (so much more insight) in the new updated version!*

Once you learn the formula to riches, you can apply it to accelerate your income into the stratosphere!

Order now, for you and your company & loved ones. Available at http://www.amazon.com, www.BarnesAndNoble.com, & any reputable bookstore.

www.ThinkRich.com/book

"Now You Can Effortlessly Transmute Commuting Down-Time To Financial Independence!"

Not Available Anywhere Else*!*!

Announcing!

The NEW Think and Grow Rich In Audio

Rare Footage!

Word-for-word reading by the author, so you understand *every* word just as it was intended!

Ted Ciuba expresses, emotes, renders, and interprets word-for-word the simple but deceptively complex information contained in the **13 named principles of *The NEW Think And Grow Rich - secrets** behind every millionaire's success* - none of which requires a thin dime.

Napoleon Hill First Discovered The Secret - Ted Ciuba Took It To New Heights In A New Age!

- Catch the true meaning and significance
- Tune into the emotions, vocal inflections, and all the other dimensions that give the *spoken* word superior communication ability over the written word!

The easiest way to fast-track your success!

Take *The NEW Think and Grow Rich*
At the "University on Wheels" - your car or transport!

www.TheNewThinkAndGrowRichAudio.com

It has a record setting history!

"Short, regular, focused, intense, intended training sessions could mean riches and fulfillment to *you!*"

Most intelligent people agree that to get ahead, you must go the extra mile. But the amazing thing is, it takes *so little* to excel!

After all, it's called the extra *mile*, not the extra *100 miles!*

Apart From Massive Intention, It Didn't Take Much

Roger Bannister
Runs sub 4 Minute Mile

Roger Bannister defied and redefined history by running the sub 4 minute mile. Exact time: 03:59.4/10's. 6 May 1954, Roger Bannister redefined human possibility by clocking in a mere 6/10's of a *second* sub 4 minutes.
And the amazing thing is that Bannister did NOT spend countless hours training… He gave it what he could in his busy pre-med schedule… A mere 30 minutes a day!!

And with that he set broke a barrier that had stood 3,000 years!

Then, within 2 1/2 years of Bannister's unachievable, record-breaking sub 4 minute mile, 18 others were doing it.

It's Your Turn! And now you can run the extra mile by tuning into a sub 4 minute length daily audio or video message with incredible motivation, insights, and training in a wide variety of fields always centered around the philosophy of *The NEW Think And Grow Rich*.

The compounding of simply sub 4 minutes every day is incredible!

You, too, can defy the status quo in **short, regular, focused, intense, intended training sessions** and **redefine what's possible for you!**

It takes so little to excel. Visit the website and get started today:

www.BigBriefMoments.com

"How Quickly Would Your Life Improve If You Began Using The Untapped 90% Of Your Brain To Bring You Wealth?!"

Revolutionary new neuroscience driven

HoloMagic Wealth Programming
Installs *The NEW Think and Grow Rich* Philosophy In You Effortlessly!

Amazing new neurosynergist® technology vaults leagues beyond ordinary hypnosis to effectuate immediate and permanent changes in your inner "wealth tracks"!

HoloMagic Wealth Programming

"Strap on your headphones, change your world!"

HoloMagic Wealth Programming is the *only* neural repatterning system in the world based on the proven principles of *The NEW Think And Grow Rich* using the patented neurosynergist® sound technology.

Dives to the depths of your *delta* subconscious, at the level where you connect with HoloCosm, and reprograms you to have and express the attitudes, strategies, and action-taking skills of the super wealthy.

Advanced thinkers, human potential experts, and the quantum and neuroscience labs affirm that the world you live in is a reflection of your inner world – the thoughts you consistently hold in your mind.

- Unleash the 90% realm of the brain that few people access and find your fortunes using the principles of *The NEW Think and Grow Rich!*…
- Put this cutting-edge, powerful, neural repatterning system to work for you!
- Visit:

www.WealthProgramming.com

"Discover The "Secret" In A Magical Mastermind Study Of The 1937 *Original Publication* Of Napoleon Hill's Success Classic, *Think And Grow Rich*!"

Achiever's MasterMind

You actively participate in working study sessions... DESIGNED WITH THE SOLE PURPOSE OF MAKING YOU WEALTHY!

www.AchieversMasterMind.com

Includes:

1. Sixteen Achiever's MasterMind Sessions In Audio
2. Achiever's MasterMind Study Chapters
1. *Achiever's MasterMind* Study Guides

Bonuses include word-for-word transcriptions!

- How to do direct imprinting into your nervous system, so that you're driven to success!
- How to harness the awesome unseen power that has created Fortunes with one secret 6-step technique. (Takes less than 5 minutes to implement.)
- The 8-part, no-fail secret the winners in the wealth game use to... Create your own "breaks"
- And much, much more!

Digital Version – Save $$$! – Audio and print files downloadable instantly!

Physical Version - so you can feed CD's into your CD player and carry the convenient notebooks with you!

www.AchieversMasterMind.com

"If You're Looking For That Decided Edge That Can Accelerate You To Riches!…"

Author of *The NEW Think And Grow Rich*, Ted Ciuba, journeyed East to forge this collaboration. The entire event was captured, and is available to you now as the…

East-West Success MasterMind
www.EastWestSuccessMasterMind.com

Share the excitement that got people tuning in from Singapore, Malaysia, China, Hong Kong, Vietnam, Korea, Philippines, Thailand, India, Australia, UK, USA, Africa, and Latin America!

The purpose of the MasterMind is quite simple...

In a MasterMind study of the success philosophy outlined in the original *Think And Grow Rich…*

- To merge the BEST of both East and West to enable any willing human being, anywhere on this planet *or any other planet or moon*, to THINK WITH INTENT…
- To control and direct your thinking to receive the *natural result* of RICHES in your life!

"One of the most important days of my life was the day I began to read Think and Grow Rich." - W. Clement Stone

"I was invited to participate in the MasterMind study of Think And Grow Rich by my friend Ted Ciuba. That 8-week program transformed my own Consciousness of Wealth... - Dan Klatt

www.EastWestSuccessMasterMind.com

Who Else Would Like To Have

The NEW Think and Grow Rich
Author Ted Ciuba
Motivate and Train Your Group?

Schedule permitting, Ted Ciuba welcomes keynote, speaking and training invitations from businesses, organizations, associations, and promoters.

The quantum performance message of *The New Think And Grow Rich* and *Sub 4 Minute Extra Mile* is perfectly suited to anyone in pursuit of money, a career, sales, and a life!

Through a brief but thorough pre-event questionnaire, Ted Ciuba makes each presentation unique to each group.

To discuss opportunities and arrangements contact our organization by email at events@holomagic.com or from the website at www.ThinkRich.com

Ted Ciuba On Stage In LA